LETTERS TO GOD

A New Musical

Book by
STUART
HAMPLE

Music by
DAVID
EVANS

Lyrics by
DOUGLAS
J. COHEN

*Based on the book by
Stuart Hample and Eric Marshall*

SAMUEL FRENCH, INC.

45 West 25th Street
NEW YORK 10010
LONDON

7623 Sunset Boulevard
HOLLYWOOD 90046
TORONTO

Book Copyright © 2005 by Stuart Hample
Lyrics Copyright © 1999, 2005 by Douglas J. Cohen

ALL RIGHTS RESERVED

CAUTION: Professionals and amateurs are hereby warned that CHILDREN'S LETTERS TO GOD, being fully protected under the copyright laws of the United States of America, the British Commonwealth, including Canada, and the other countries of the Copyright Union, is subject to a royalty, and anyone presenting the play without the consent of the owners or their authorized agents will be liable to the penalties by law provided.

Amateurs wishing to arrange for the production of CHILDREN'S LETTERS TO GOD must make application to SAMUEL FRENCH, INC., at 45 West 25th Street, New York, NY 10010-2751, giving the following particulars:

(1) The name of the town and theatre or hall in which the proposed production will be presented.

(2) The maximum seating capacity of the theatre or hall.

(3) Scale of ticket prices; and

(4) The number of performances intended and the dates thereof.

Upon receipt of these particulars SAMUEL FRENCH, INC., will quote the amateur terms and availability.

Stock royalty and availability quoted on application to SAMUEL FRENCH, INC., at 45 West 25th Street, New York, NY 10010-2751.

For all other rights than those stipulated above, apply to **Douglas & Kopelman Artists, Inc.**, 393 West 49th Street, Suite 5G, New York, NY 10019 and Zip Productions & Management, inc., 26 Norman Road, Montclair, NJ 07043.

An orchestration consisting of Piano/Vocal Score and Chorus Books will be loaned two months prior to the production ONLY on receipt of the royalty quoted for all performances, the rental fee and a refundable deposit. The deposit will be refunded on the safe return to SAMUEL FRENCH, INC. of all materials loaned for the production.

No one shall commit or authorize any act or omission by which the copyright of, or the right to copyright, this play may be impaired.

No one shall make any changes in this play for the purposes of production.

Publication of this play does not imply availability for performance. Both amateurs and professionals considering a production are strongly advised in their own interests to apply to Samuel French, Inc., for written permission before starting rehearsals, advertising, or booking a theatre.

No part of this book may be reproduced, stored in a retrieval system, or transmitted in any form, by any means, now known or yet to be invented, including mechanical, electronic, photocopying, recording, videotaping, or otherwise, without the prior permission of the publisher.

Printed in U.S.A.
ISBN 0 573 63215 4

IMPORTANT BILLING AND CREDIT REQUIREMENTS

All producers of CHILDREN'S LETTERS TO GOD *must* give credit to the author of the work in all programs distributed in connection with performances of the Work, and in all instances in which the title of the Work appears for the purposes of advertising, publicizing or otherwise exploiting a production thereof, including, without limitation, programs, souvenir books and playbills. The name of the Author *must* appear on a separate line in which no other matter appears, immediately following the title of the Work, and *must* be in size of type not less than 50% of the size used for the title of the Work.

Billing must be substantially as follows:

(NAME OF PRODUCER)

Presents

CHILDREN'S LETTERS TO GOD (100%)

Book by	Music by	Lyrics by (50%)
STUART HAMPLE	DAVID EVANS	DOUGLAS J. COHEN

Based on the book by Stuart Hample and Eric Marshall (50%)

Originally Produced by Carolyn Rossi Copeland Productions, Inc. and The Lamb's Theatre Co., Ltd. (25%)

Developed at the Lark Play Development Center, New York City (15%)

Originally presented in the Developmental Reading Series at The York Theatre Company, James Morgan, Artistic Director (15%)

LAMB'S THEATRE

CAROLYN ROSSI COPELAND

and

MARIE B. CORPORATION
BROADWAY OVERSEAS MANAGEMENT

present

CHILDREN'S LETTERS TO GOD

Book by	Music by	Lyrics by
STUART HAMPLE	DAVID EVANS	DOUGLAS J. COHEN

based on the book by Stuart Hample and Eric Marshall

Starring
GERARD CANONICO JIMMY DIEFFENBACH LIBBIE JACOBSON
SARA KAPNER ANDREW ZUTTY

Set Design	Lighting Design	Sound Design
ANNA LOUIZOS	KIRK BOOKMAN	PETER HYLENSKI

Costume Design	Production Stage Manager	Press Representative
GAIL BRASSARD	JASON SUTTON	KEITH SHERMAN & ASSOCIATES

Marketing
LEANNE SCHANZER
PROMOTIONS, INC.

Musical Direction
LARRY PRESSGROVE

General Management
R. ERIN CRAIG

Production Management
AURORA PRODUCTIONS

Musical Staging
PATRICIA WILCOX

Direction by
STAFFORD ARIMA

In Association with The Lamb's Theatre Company, Ltd.

THE CHARACTERS

JOANNA, 13 — Bright, responsible, and romantic, she is often forced to take care of her intrusive little brother, Kicker, who at times drives everyone crazy. She's in the same class as Brett, on whom she has her heart set.

KICKER, 9 — Joanna's brother; imaginative; questions everything; often feels powerless because he's the youngest and the smallest in the group.

BRETT, 13 — A doubter, sometimes a tad cocky to cover his insecurity, parents divorced. His prized possession is a baseball cap covered with a variety of pins from special places which he wears at all times.

IRIS, 11 — Passionately in love with her pet turtle, Arnold. Tends to over dramatize herself and has a secret crush on Brett.

THEO, 11 — About to celebrate his 12th birthday. Totally inept physically but is happy that he is not as physically inept as Kicker. Would fervently like to be an athlete/hero. Wears glasses.

[The parts will be played by a multicultural cast of age-appropriate children; for example, in our New York production, Iris happened to be Asian, so we changed her last name to Chang. You should feel free to make similar substitutions. The ages may range from 7 to 15, according to the actual ages of the actors.]

FURTHER CASTING OPTIONS

While CHILDREN'S LETTERS TO GOD was originally written to be performed by five kids ages 7-15, it is possible to expand the cast with more performers: these additional cast members should only be assigned letters and solo lyrics that are not character specific.

In the following numbers, where the entire cast sings (as indicated by the word ALL), feel free to add the additional voices:

"QUESTIONS/QUESTIONS"
"LIKE EVERYBODY ELSE"
"QUESTIONS FOR THE RAIN"
"A SIMPLE HOLIDAY SONG"
"WHEN I AM IN CHARGE"
"DAYDREAMS"
"HOW COME?"
"I KNOW"

The show can also be performed by a cast of young adults if age-appropriate children are not available.

In addition, it is possible to enlist a local church, synagogue, school or community group to participate in the show by joining in the singing of the final song, "I KNOW."

A NOTE ABOUT "TITLES"

We have suggested projecting "titles" throughout the show to preserve the sense of chapter headings that appear in the book, CHILDREN'S LETTERS TO GOD. In the Lamb's Theatre production off-Broadway, we were unable to do this due to a thrust stage. But in a proscenium house, titles could be used successfully.

Titles are optional and do not have to be "projected" by light onto a screen: they can also be creatively revealed on parts of the set, for example. We encourage productions to be imaginative.

THE PHYSICAL PRODUCTION

CHILDREN'S LETTERS TO GOD can be done with minimal props and scene changes and a set that allows the action to be fluid. The various locations (school, Kicker's bedroom, party, etc...) can be indicated minimally or more extensively, according to the director's vision.

SONGS

1. PROLOGUE/QUESTIONS, QUESTIONS........................Company
2. THIRTEEN..BRETT
3. ARNOLD...IRIS and Company
4. LIKE EVERYBODY ELSE...............................THEO and Company
5. QUESTIONS FOR THE RAIN............................IRIS and Company
6. ANTS..KICKER
7. A SIMPLE HOLIDAY SONG...Company
8. SIX HOURS AS A PRINCESS..JOANNA
9. AN ONLY CHILD..KICKER and JOANNA
10. WHEN I AM IN CHARGE...Company
11. DAYDREAMS:
      I WILL NOT DREAM IN CLASS............JOANNA and IRIS
      DAYDREAMS - PART ONE......................................Company
      ARE YOU HAPPY WITH ME?................................Company
      WYOMING...BRETT
      DAYDREAMS - PART TWO....................................Company
12. KICKER BROWN..THEO
13. SILLY OLD HAT...BRETT
14. HOW COME?...Company
15. I KNOW..Company
16. Bows – I KNOW (reprise)...Company

ACT I

(In the dark, we hear children's voices:)

BRETT. Dear God, If you're so famous, how come you're never on T.V.?
KICKER. Dear God, Please send Dennis Clark to a different camp this year.
IRIS. Dear God, How did you know you were God?
JOANNA. Dear God, Thank you for the baby brother, but what I prayed for was a puppy.
THEO. Dear God, How come you did all those miracles in the old days and don't do any now?

(Pin-spot on JOANNA, who sings:)

Song: *"PROLOGUE"*

JOANNA.
IN THE BEGINNING...
GOD CREATED THE HEAVENS
AND THE EARTH.
HE SET THE WORLD SPINNING
SO WE CAN CONCLUDE —

KICKER. Dear God, Please make my sister prettier so she can get married.

JOANNA.
(A bit annoyed)
THAT HE CREATED BROTHERS

WHO SOMETIMES INTRUDE!

KICKER. Sorrrr-ry.

JOANNA.
BUT FIRST HE ADDED FLOWERS
AND FISHES IN THE SEA...
AND BIRDS AND ANIMALS
IN ALL THEIR GLORY —

IRIS. Dear God, Is Pastor Bowen*a friend of yours or do you just know him through business?

JOANNA.
WOULD YOU RATHER TELL THIS STORY?

IRIS. Okay!
THEN HE MADE MAN AND WOMAN
WHO BROUGHT FORTH CHILDREN —

THEO. Dear God ...What does begat mean? Nobody will tell me.
BRETT. *(Whispering to THEO.)* Two people making babies.
THEO. Ewwww! That's gross!

JOANNA.
AND THEIR CHILDREN
HAD CHILDREN

IRIS. Dear God, I bet you can't name the capitals of every state. I can!
BRETT. Hey God, A lot of people say bad things with your name in it, but I never do.
KICKER. Dear God, Did you have as much trouble learning Hebrew as I am?

ALL.
AND THESE CHILDREN
HAVE LOTS OF QUESTIONS!

*Can be replaced by the name of a local clergy person.

CHILDREN'S LETTERS TO GOD

Song: *"QUESTIONS/QUESTIONS"*

(Upbeat music sounds)
QUESTIONS, QUESTIONS
THINGS WE GOTTA KNOW —
EVERYTHING FROM

BRETT.
ARE YOU REAL?

IRIS.
TO HOW YOU MAKE IT SNOW...

ALL.
ANSWERS, ANSWERS
NEVER SEEM TO COME!

JOANNA.
WHY DO PEOPLE HAVE TO DIE?

THEO.
AND WHO INVENTED GUM?

IRIS/JOANNA.
MAYBE YOU ARE HARD OF HEARING

KICKER/THEO.
MAYBE YOU DON'T REALLY CARE

JOANNA.
MAYBE YOU ARE ON VACATION

BRETT.
MAYBE YOU'RE NOT REALLY THERE

ALL.
MAYBE WE'RE TALKING TO THE AIR!

LETTERS, LETTERS —

MAYBE IF WE WRITE,
THEN WE'LL GET AN ANSWER
IF YOUR SCHEDULE'S NOT TOO TIGHT.

LOTS OF LETTERS,
THAT'S A WAY TO START.
LETTERS FROM WHAT'S ON OUR MIND
AND LETTERS FROM THE HEART...

   BRETT.
THINGS WE'D NEVER ASK OUR PARENTS —

   KICKER.
LIKE WHAT ABOUT THE BIRDS AND BEES?

   THEO.
AND WHY IS SUNDAY SCHOOL ON SUNDAY?

   ALL.
SO, GOD,
HOW ABOUT IT?
TELL US, PLEASE...

   IRIS/JOANNA/KICKER.
HOW DO YOU MAKE THE WATER FREEZE?

   THEO/BRETT.
WHY DO THE SWISS MAKE BETTER CHEESE?

   ALL.
WHO SAYS "GOD BLESS YOU" WHEN YOU SNEEZE?

QUESTIONS, QUESTIONS
RUNNING THROUGH MY BRAIN

   KICKER/IRIS.
DO YOU LOOK LIKE HERCULES...?

JOANNA/THEO/BRETT.
OR MORE LIKE CELLOPHANE?

ALL.
AND AFTER YOU ANSWER THESE
WE'RE NOT THROUGH —
GOD, YOU HAVE A LOT OF EXPLAINING
TO DO!

(Transition of lights and music. A title appears:)

[Complaints & Doubts]

(The stage lights pick out KICKER in his "room". It's a mess – a heap of his clothing and toys.)

JOANNA. KICKER BROWN! Your room is a mess!
KICKER. Dear God, My sister Joanna thinks she's God. Boy, is she wrong!
JOANNA. You better clean it up fast, or mom says you can't go to Theo's birthday party.
KICKER. Dear God... I will clean up my room if you will send me a pony. Is it a deal? Your friend, Kicker.
JOANNA. Start picking up, Kicker!
KICKER. You're not the boss of me!
JOANNA. No, but I'm bigger than you.
KICKER. It's too hard to do it alone. *(Pleading)* You have to help me.
JOANNA. Okay, munchkin, we'll do it together. *(She notices her binoculars.)* Hey, what are you doing with my binoculars? Were you spying on me and Brett?!
KICKER. No.
JOANNA. *(She shoots him an accusatory glance.)* Kiiiiiiick-er? You were, weren't you!
KICKER. Um...I forget...
(Cornered, he runs to the wings.)
MOM!! JOANNA MESSED UP MY ROOM!

(He exits fast!)

JOANNA. Dear God, It must be hard for you to love everybody in the world. I only have one brother and I can't do it.

(The lights change to a scene outside. BRETT appears, carrying a gift. He wears his baseball cap with buttons and badges on it.)

Song: *"THIRTEEN"*

BRETT.
CAKE AND ICE CREAM AND PARTY FAVORS.
PLAYING GAMES WITH FRIENDS – BIG WOW.
WHY IS IT THINGS I LOVED LAST YEAR
SEEM SO STUPID NOW?

DAD MOVED OUT ON NOVEMBER SEVENTH;
I GREW AN INCH-AND-A-HALF LAST SPRING.
SO MANY CHANGES IN ONE YEAR...
WONDER WHAT NEXT YEAR WILL BRING?

TURN THIRTEEN
AND THINGS GO CRAZY –
FEELING LIKE A TOTAL FREAK!
VOICE IS GETTING LOWER,
SCHOOL YEAR'S GETTING SLOWER.
AND I'M SHAVING EVERY OTHER WEEK!

DAD MOVED OUT ON NOVEMBER SEVENTH;
MOM THREW OUT HER WEDDING RING.
SO MANY CHANGES IN ONE YEAR...
WONDER WHAT NEXT YEAR WILL BRING?

(JOANNA enters carrying a gift. She runs to catch up with him.)

JOANNA. Brett!
BRETT. Hey! Joanna.
JOANNA. Wait for me.
BRETT. Alright, if you're nice, I'll let you walk me to Theo's birthday party.

JOANNA. At last my life is complete!
BRETT. Don't mention it.
JOANNA. If I know you, you're giving Theo something real, like, strange, right? Lemme see...

(She tries to grab his gift but BRETT pulls away.)

BRETT. It's top secret.
JOANNA. Now — what would somebody with your twisted brain — covered in that weird hat — give another person for a birthday gift?
BRETT. Forget it. You'll never guess.
JOANNA. If you want to know the actual truth, I...don't...care!

(He grabs her present and runs off. She chases him, yelling.)

JOANNA. Brett Williams! Gimme that!

(BRETT runs to the party followed closely by JOANNA; THEO and KICKER are already there.)

BRETT. *(Handing the two gifts to THEO.)* Theo, you're such a great guy, I brought you two presents!
JOANNA. *(Grabbing her gift and offering it.)* One's from me!
BRETT. Open mine first!
THEO. *(THEO stands stunned having been forced into a private feud; he decides to grab BRETT'S present. JOANNA sits with her brother.)* A baseball mitt? Thanks, but I stink at baseball!
BRETT. You have to work at it, Dude. You'll get better.
THEO. How can I do that? I need a coach to teach me.
BRETT. Hard to find.
THEO. How about you?
BRETT. Maybe as a special birthday bonus.
THEO. Really?
BRETT. No promises.
THEO. Hey, cool, dude!

(THEO raises his hand to high-five BRETT, but he misses when BRETT turns and walks towards the birthday cake. IRIS enters furious, clutching her Birthday invitation and carrying her turtle, ARNOLD.)

IRIS. Theo, I just came to tell you that I am not coming to your party!

THEO. But, you're already here!

IRIS. *(Pulls out invitation.)* I'm leaving because your dumb invitation says "No Turtles Allowed."

THEO. You're allowed. But not your dumb turtle.

IRIS. Too bad. Because if Arnold is not allowed, then I am leaving.

THEO. Birthdays are for people, not pets.

IRIS. Which shows how little you know, since it is a fact of nature that Arnold is more than just a pet!

Song: *"ARNOLD"*

IT'S NOT LIKE HE CAN FETCH A STICK
OR HOP OR PURR
OR EVEN LICK.
BUT GOD HAD BETTER THINGS IN MIND, YOU SEE,
THE DAY THAT HE BROUGHT ARNOLD TO ME...

(IRIS holds up the turtle.)

THEO. I said no turtles!

IRIS.
ARNOLD KNOWS
IT'S OKAY TO TAKE TIME,
IT'S OKAY TO STUDY A BLADE OF GRASS.
ARNOLD KNOWS
WHEN I'VE GOT SHOW 'N TELL
I CAN ALWAYS TAKE HIM TO CLASS.

ARNOLD KNOWS
HOW TO LISTEN REAL HARD —
IF I SHARE A SECRET, HE'LL NEVER TALK.
AND ARNOLD KNOWS
TO RETREAT IN HIS SHELL
AND DO HIS COOL IMPRESSION OF A ROCK.

THEO. Hey! Is this my birthday or what?

IRIS.
(KICKER, BRETT & JOANNA ECHO)
HE'S SLOW
SO I KNOW JUST WHERE TO FIND HIM.
AND HE MOVES LIKE PEOPLE DO
WHEN THEY GET OLD.
SO WHO CARES IF HE'S NOT SPEEDY AS A ROCKET?
HOW MANY PETS CAN FIT INSIDE YOUR POCKET?

ALL.
(Except THEO)
ARNOLD KNOWS

IRIS.
WHEN I DON'T WEAR A SMILE

JOANNA.
IT'S BECAUSE A SMILE DOESN'T FIT YOUR MOOD.

KICKER /BRETT/ JOANNA.
ARNOLD KNOWS

IRIS.
THAT I LIKE WHAT HE LIKES

KICKER.
BUT YOU'LL NEVER LIKE TURTLE FOOD.

IRIS.
AND ARNOLD KNOWS
HOW TO BLEND RIGHT IN.
HE WON'T SCREAM FOR ATTENTION
TO PROVE HE'S SMART...
AND IF HE MOVES AT A SLOWER PACE,
ARNOLD KNOWS

ALL.
(Except THEO)

ARNOLD KNOWS

IRIS.
MY ARNOLD KNOWS
HOW TO FIND A PLACE
IN MY HEART.

THEO. Okay. Your slimy turtle can stay.
KICKER. Great. *(Cookie Monster voice.)* Chocolate cake! Me love it!
IRIS. *(Holds ARNOLD, her turtle, near the cake.)* Cut a piece for Arnold.
THEO. Turtles don't eat cake.
IRIS. Arnold hasn't been himself lately. He needs a treat.
THEO. I just got a treat! Brett's gonna be my baseball coach! Thanks, Dude!

(He raises his hand for BRETT to high-five, and misses.)

KICKER. He can't even do a high-five. What a geek.
JOANNA. Kicker, that's mean.
KICKER. So? Everybody says he's a geek.
JOANNA. You apologize.
KICKER. I'm sorry you're a geek.
JOANNA. Kicker!
KICKER. I'm sorry.
THEO. It's okay. I am a geek.
JOANNA. Theo, you are not a geek just because you can't do a high-five. Now stop sulking and make your wish.
THEO. *(From the heart.)* I wish...I didn't drop a fly ball every single time...and go on my rollerblades without falling over...and not have this stupid baby face so I look about five years old...I wish I could be like everybody else.

(He starts to blow out the candle.)

JOANNA. Theo! Why would you want to waste a perfectly good wish on that?

Song: *"LIKE EVERYBODY ELSE"*

JOANNA.
IF EVERYONE YOU KNEW
WAS JUST LIKE EVERYBODY ELSE...

KICKER.
THEY PROBABLY WOULD NEVER HAVE OLYMPICS
(They all look at him a tad confused.)
'CAUSE IF A HUNDRED PEOPLE RAN
THE HUNDRED METER RACE,
WE'D NEED A HUNDRED MEDALS
FOR THEY'D ALL COME IN FIRST PLACE!

JOANNA.
IF EVERYONE YOU KNEW
WAS JUST LIKE EVERYBODY ELSE,
YOU COULDN'T TELL MY BROTHER
FROM A TURTLE.

IRIS.
EXCEPT ONE LIKES THE WATER

JOANNA.
AND THE OTHER HATES A BATH.

BRETT.
ONE GIVES OFF A FUNNY SMELL,

JOANNA.
THE OTHER STINKS AT MATH.

KICKER. Hey!

JOANNA.
BOTH COULD USE A HARDER SHELL

IRIS.
TIME WILL TELL,
IT'S JUST AS WELL

ALL.
(Except THEO)
THAT EVERYONE YOU KNOW
IS NOT LIKE EVERYBODY ELSE.

IF EVERYONE YOU KNEW
WAS JUST LIKE EVERYBODY ELSE...

BRETT.
WE PROBABLY WOULD NEVER GO TO MOVIES —
YOU WOULDN'T WANT TO SPEND YOUR MONEY
JUST TO SIT AND SEE

ALL.
(Except THEO)
PEOPLE WHO ALL LOOK AND ACT THE SAME AS
YOU AND ME!

IRIS.
LIFE WOULD BE AN AWFUL BORE —

ADD JOANNA.
WHAT IS MORE

ADD BRETT.
BE THANKFUL YOU'RE

ALL.
(Except THEO)
THEO
AND YOU'RE SOMEONE
UNLIKE EVERYBODY ELSE!

THEO.
BUT IF I ONLY HAD A BODY
THAT NOBODY WOULD TEASE...

IRIS.
I WISH I DIDN'T HAVE BIG EARS,
BUT SO WHAT?

KICKER.
OH, GIVE ME LONGER LEGS

JOANNA.
WITHOUT KNOBBY KNEES.

BRETT.
I HAVE A GIANT BIRTHMARK RIGHT ON MY BUTT.

IRIS.
SO THEO, STOP YOUR CRYING AND TRYING
TO PLEASE...

JOANNA.
BE PLEASED WITH WHO YOU ARE —

ALL.
(Except THEO)
A ONE-OF-A-KIND STAR!

THEO.
I'M ONE-OF-A-KIND!

ALL.
OH, IF EVERYONE YOU KNEW
WAS JUST LIKE EVERYBODY ELSE...

THEO.
I GUESS THERE'D BE A MILLION, TRILLION THEO'S.

JOANNA.
AND UNLIKE EVERY SNOWFLAKE
EVERYONE WOULD BE THE SAME,

BRETT.
AND WHEN I'D CALL, "HEY, THEO!"
THEY'D ALL ANSWER TO YOUR NAME.

IRIS.
YOU COULDN'T TELL WHO'S REAL OR FAKE,

KICKER.
I COULD TAKE YOUR PIECE OF CAKE!

ALL.
(Except THEO)
NO MISTAKE ABOUT IT,
CAN'T YOU SEE...

BRETT.
A SNAKE'S NOT MEANT TO FLY,
A BIRD'S NOT MEANT TO SWIM.

KICKER.
I'M GLAD THAT I'M NOT HER —

JOANNA.
I'M THRILLED THAT I'M NOT HIM.

IRIS.
BE HAPPY YOU ARE YOU

IRIS/ BRETT.
'CAUSE TWO OF YOU WON'T DO

ALL.
(Except THEO)
AND THAT GOES DOUBLE IF THERE WERE A FEW!
FOR IF EVERYONE YOU KNEW
WAS JUST LIKE EVERYONE YOU KNEW
THEN IT WOULD BE OUR BIRTHDAY TOO!
"HAPPY BIRTHDAY TO US" –

THEO.
NO ...
ME!

ALL.
(Except THEO, Overlaping with THEO'S held note.)
"HAPPY BIRTHDAY TO YOU!!!"

(Transition of lights and music. A title appears:)

[Forces of Nature]

IRIS. Dear God, do plastic flowers make you mad? I would be if I made the real ones.

KICKER. Dear God, why do you always make the grass green And the sky blue? Are those the only colors you have?

THEO. We read that Thomas Edison invented light. But in Sunday school they said YOU did it. So I bet he stole your idea.

IRIS. *(Bends down to look at something)* Look, a spider caught a fly.

KICKER. Yecccch! I hate flies. Also spiders.

IRIS. They're God's creatures, just like we are. Just like Arnold.

KICKER. I don't care whose creatures they are! Keep 'em away from me!

BRETT. God doesn't make flies and spiders. They just are!

JOANNA. You are so clueless it's pathetic!

BRETT. He doesn't make everything!

(We hear thunder)

JOANNA. Where do you think that comes from?

(It suddenly rains. All but IRIS run for cover.)

BRETT. *(Shields his hat from the rain.)* Oh, NO!!!

IRIS. *(She looks skyward, twirls happily, arms out.)* Rain! I LOVE it!

BRETT. My hat's getting wet!

JOANNA. What is it with you and that hat?

BRETT. It's private, okay?

KICKER. Dear God ...Last week it rained so much it was almost like Noah's Ark. But I'm glad it wasn't...'cause you could only take two of things, remember? And we have three cats!

Song: *"QUESTIONS FOR THE RAIN"*

IRIS.
WHAT DID PEOPLE DO BEFORE UMBRELLAS?

THEO.
DO FISH HAVE A CLUE THAT IT'S RAINING?

BRETT.
WHY'S IT ALWAYS FALL ON
SOME IMPORTANT BASEBALL GAME?

JOANNA.
HOW COME FLOWERS GROW...

KICKER.
BUT I JUST STAY THE SAME?

THEO.
CAN'T YOU MAKE IT SO IT SKIPS THE WEEKENDS?

IRIS.
DOES RAIN MEAN THAT YOU MIGHT BE CRYING?

JOANNA.
IS IT LIKE THE SNOW:
ARE NO TWO RAINDROPS ALIKE?

THEO.
WHY DOES IT TURN GRASS GREEN?

BRETT.
BUT IT JUST RUSTS MY BIKE?

ALL.
QUESTIONS FOR THE RAIN
WHILE THUNDERCLAPS ARE RINGING

THEO.
WHY DOES DADDY CURSE IT...

JOANNA.
BUT IN MOVIES THEY START SINGING?

ALL.
WHY'S IT ALWAYS CLEAR?
IS IT TEARS DISGUISED?

KICKER.
IS IT SAFE TO DRINK?

BRETT.
SHOULD WE WAIT TILL IT'S PASTEURIZED?

ALL.
QUESTIONS FOR THE RAIN —
SOME THINGS I SOMETIMES WONDER...
WHICH IS IT MORE FOND OF:
THE LIGHTNING OR THE THUNDER?

IRIS.
DOES THE SUN GET WET
OR DOES THE RAIN PASS RIGHT THROUGH IT?

THEO.
WHEN YOU MAKE IT RAIN
HOW DO YOU KNOW HOW LONG TO DO IT?

ALL.
QUESTIONS FOR THE —

IRIS.
(SCREAMS)

    JOANNA. *(Rushes to her.)* What's the matter?
    IRIS. Arnold's not moving! I think he's...dead!
    KICKER. Really? Dead? Wow! How can you tell?
    BRETT. Turtles look dead even when they're alive!
    JOANNA. Oh, Brett!
    BRETT. *(Leans down over ARNOLD.)* Let me take his pulse.

KICKER. I never saw anything dead before — except an ant.
BRETT. *(Looks at ARNOLD.)* Yep. He's dead all right.
JOANNA. Some people think we live after we die.
BRETT. Forget it.
IRIS. *(Places ARNOLD on the ground.)* If we live after we die, why do we have to die then?
JOANNA. Maybe it was his time.
IRIS. It's not fair! If I was God I would let everybody's turtle live forever!
BRETT. Nobody lives forever.
KICKER. Dear God, what is it like when you die? I just want to know, I don't want to do it.
JOANNA. It's sad, but you were lucky you had such a great turtle.
IRIS. Dear God...Instead of letting people die and having to make new ones, why don't you just keep the ones you got now?

ALL.
(Except IRIS)
GOD, WE GIVE YOU THANKS
JUST LIKE ON THANKSGIVING...

IRIS.
BUT I'D BE MORE THANKFUL
IF MY FRIEND WAS LIVING.

THEO.
WAS HE IN MUCH PAIN?
HE LOOKS AWFUL GREEN.

BRETT.
ARNOLD WAS A TURTLE —
THEY ARE ALWAYS GREEN!

IRIS.
OH, WHY DID YOU TAKE HIM IN HIS PRIME?!

THEO.
WAS HE REALLY THAT YOUNG?

IRIS.
I'D SAY HE WAS MAYBE THREE OR SO —
WITH TURTLES IT'S KIND OF HARD TO KNOW.

JOANNA. And so we lay to rest Iris Burns' beloved turtle *(Beat)* Arnold Burns.

KICKER.
IS THERE SUCH A THING AS TURTLE HEAVEN?

THEO.
WILL ARNOLD COME BACK AS A RABBIT?

IRIS.
WILL I EVER SEE MY LITTLE FRIEND AGAIN?
P.S. THERE'S NO RUSH —   *(Alternate lyric if IRIS is older:)*
REMEMBER I'M JUST TEN.   I'M ONLY TWELVE, AMEN.

KICKER.
IF HE'S WET, WILL HE GET
PNEUMONIA?

THEO.
WHY AM I HUNGRY FOR FRENCH FRIES?

JOANNA.
EVEN THOUGH HE'S GONE,
IS IT STILL HELPFUL TO PRAY?

BRETT.
IF THE RAIN WON'T STOP —
WILL ARNOLD FLOAT AWAY...?

(JOANNA shoots him a disapproving glance.)

ALL.
QUESTIONS FOR THE RAIN
I'M HAPPY TO HAVE KNOWN HIM

IRIS.
DON'T MEAN TO COMPLAIN BUT

IS IT TOO LATE TO CLONE HIM?

ALL.
(Except IRIS)
HE WILL ALWAYS BE TURTLE NUMBER ONE,
THE VERY BEST OF FRIENDS —
WE SURE HAD LOTS OF FUN.

IRIS.
THANK YOU FOR MY ARNOLD...

(The sky clears and sunlight breaks through.)

ALL.
AND THANK YOU FOR THE SUN.

(We hear sounds of car horns.)

> **JOANNA.** C'mon Kicker, mom and dad are here. Bye, Brett.
> **THEO.** See ya!
> **BRETT.** *(To JOANNA)* Later.
> **KICKER.** *(Runs toward "car")* Hey, Mom – I saw a real live dead turtle!

(Exits with JOANNA.)

> **IRIS.** Brett? D'you need a ride?
> **BRETT.** No thanks. My mom's coming. I think.
> **IRIS.** Aren't you sure?
> **BRETT.** Not really, 'cause ever since they got divorced and my dad moved out, she's been kind of losing it.
> **IRIS.** *(Not wanting him to be disappointed.)* Sure you don't wanna come with us?
> **BRETT.** Nah...I'm cool. *(IRIS starts to leave.)* Hey, Iris — you okay about Arnold?
> **IRIS.** Yeah...thanks for asking...that's really sweet...well, bye, Brett. *(She runs to the "car", suddenly losing it.)* Mommy...! Arnold ...diiiiiiiiiiiiiiiied!!!!!
> **BRETT.** Dear God, how do you feel about people who don't believe in you? *(A beat)* Somebody else wants to know.

(Transition of lights and music. A pin-spot picks out each KID as he/she speaks a letter.)

    JOANNA. Dear God, do animals believe in you or is there somebody else for them?
    IRIS. Did you mean for giraffes to look so funny or was that a mistake?
    THEO. I hope ants aren't special because we squish them all the time.

Song: *"ANTS"*

KICKER.
HOW I LOVE TO SQUISH ANTS!
HOW I LOVE TO STOMP ANTS!
WHO GAVE 'EM PERMISSION TO CRAWL UP MY PANTS?!

HOW I LOVE TO SMASH ANTS!
HOW I LOVE TO MASH ANTS!
THAT IS WHY I GOTTA DO MY SQUISHY ANTS' DANCE!

HOW I HATE ANY BUG,
EVERY SPIDER AND SLUG.
EVERY TIME I SEE ONE, I WANNA YELL "UGH!"
IT'S ALWAYS KIND OF MESSY WHEN YOU SQUISH 'EM ON A RUG —
BUT I LOVE TO SQUISH ANTS!

(He does a little ant-squishing dance. BRETT and JOANNA enter with a large rubber ball.)

    JOANNA. Hey, Munchkin.
    KICKER. Where are you guys going?
    BRETT. To check out the new roller coaster.
    KICKER. Can I go?
    JOANNA. You're too little.
    BRETT. And too shrimpy. Hey, Kicker, you're good at kicking people. Let's see if you can catch.

(Tosses the ball to JOANNA over KICKER'S head.)

JOANNA. Yeah, Kicker, catch!

(Tosses the ball back over KICKER. BRETT bounces the ball off of KICKER'S back.)

KICKER. Ow!
BRETT. Wow! What a great backboard!
JOANNA. Hey! Be nice to my little brother!
KICKER. Yeah, Dorkhead!
JOANNA. *I'm* the only one who's allowed to torture him!

(She shoves KICKER towards BRETT. He puts kicker into a head lock and gives him a "noogie")

BRETT. Say Mercy. Say it!
KICKER. Mercy!
BRETT. Thank you!

(BRETT and JOANNA exit laughing.)

KICKER.
I WILL NEVER SQUISH ANTS —
I WILL ONLY HELP ANTS.
JUST LIKE LITTLE PEOPLE, ANTS DESERVE A CHANCE!

REMEMBER, EV'RY BUG
DEEP DOWN JUST WANTS A HUG.

NO ONE LIKES BEING CREPT ON,
BUT IT'S WORSE GETTING STEPPED ON.
I WILL NEVER, NEVER, NEVER, NEVER, NEVER, NEVER, EVER SQUISH ANTS!

(Transition of lights and music. THEO and JOANNA enter.)

THEO. C'mon, Iris, we're going to the zoo.

(IRIS enters, still in mourning for the deceased Arnold; she wears all black, including a black turtleneck.)

    IRIS. Not me. I will never look at another animal in my entire life.
    JOANNA. Why not?
    IRIS. Because I am in mourning for the only animal I ever truly loved — Arnold, my late turtle. And that is why, in honor of Arnold's blessed memory, I am dressed all in black, and wearing my turtleneck.
    THEO. Why don't you just get another turtle?
    IRIS. Because I wouldn't be able to love another turtle as much as I loved Arnold.
    JOANNA. So then...get some other...not-turtle-ish kind of animal.
    IRIS. *(Self-dramatizing.)* Never! Now if you'll excuse me, I have to be alone with my memories.
    JOANNA. Iris!

(She rushes off pursuing her friend. BRETT enters, crosses rapidly. THEO, with mitt and ball, calls out to him.)

    THEO. Can you do it now?
    BRETT. Do? What??
    THEO. Coach me how to catch.
    BRETT. Sorry, Theo, I'm late for someplace.
    THEO. *(Calls after him.)* Then when?
    BRETT. *(Leaving)* I'll find you, buddy...
    THEO. *(In frustration.)* I hope it's before snow covers the baseball field! *(...and exits fast!)*

(A title appears:)

[Holidays & Other Torments]

(IRIS, JOANNA, and KICKER enter dressed in winter hats and scarves.)

    IRIS. Dear God, Why can't there be another holiday between Christmas and Easter. There is nothing good in there now.
    JOANNA. Dear God, our teacher read us the part where all the Jews went through the water and got away. Keep up the good work. P.S.

I'm Jewish.

KICKER. Dear God, with so many different religions, don't you get mixed up sometimes?

Song: *"A SIMPLE HOLIDAY SONG"*

IRIS.
(Encourages the others to join in)
FA LA LA LA LA LA FA LA LA!

LET'S SING A SIMPLE HOLIDAY SONG:
FA LA LA FA LA LA LA LA LA!

BABY JESUS BORN IN A MANGER –

ALL.
(Except IRIS)
NOT SO FAST:
I MAY BE A STRANGER
TO YOUR KIND OF HOLIDAY SONG

IRIS.
SING A SIMPLE HOLIDAY SONG:
FA LA LA FA LA LA –

JOANNA.
(Cutting her off)
NOT FOR ME.
SPINNING DREIDELS, DANCING A HORAH,
CHANT IN HEBREW, LIGHT THE MENORAH:
BARUCH ATA ADONAI ELOHEINU MELECH HAOLAM...
THAT'S OUR SIMPLE HOLIDAY SONG.

THEO.
BUT WHAT OF KWANZAA?
YOU CAN'T FORGET KWANZAA.
FROM AN OLD SWAHILI PHRASE,
IT LASTS I THINK FOR SEVEN DAYS.

IRIS.
(Competitively)
MINE LASTS FOR TWELVE —

JOANNA.
MINE LASTS FOR EIGHT.

BRETT.
AT LEAST YOU GET TO CELEBRATE!
(With feigned enthusiasm:)
SING A SIMPLE HOLIDAY SONG:
FA LA LA FA LA LA LA LA – LA!
MOM ON CHRISTMAS,
DAD IS ON NEW YEAR'S –
I DRINK CIDER,
HE HAS A FEW BEERS.
YOU GET PRETTY USED TO IT ALL
WHEN YOU'RE A HOLIDAY VOLLEY BALL.

KICKER.
SING A SIMPLE HOLIDAY SONG:
FA–LA–LA–FA–LA–LA–LA-LA!
SING OF JOY THIS SEASON FOR GIVING —
ALL THOSE GIFTS ARE REASON FOR LIVING!

ALL.
HALLELUJAH!
HALLELUJAH!

KICKER.
ALL IS TOYS "R" US DOT-COM,
All IS BRIGHT.

IRIS.
SO SING OF KING OF KINGS

THEO.
CELEBRATIONS
HARVEST CELEBRATIONS

JOANNA.
THE FESTIVAL OF LIGHTS

BRETT.
BUS STATIONS —
GO GREYHOUND!

KICKER.
OF SANTA CLAUS

ALL.
AND WINTER VACATIONS!
SING A SIMPLE HOLIDAY SONG...

IRIS.
FA LA LA FA LA LA LA LA LA

THEO.
NGUZO SABA, KWANZA

JOANNA.
BORUCH ATA ADONAI ELOHEINU MELECH   *(Simultaneously)*
HAOLAM...

KICKER.
MACY'S, SANTA, FAO SCHWARZ

BRETT.
MOM, DAD, GREYHOUND.

ALL.
IT'S NOT EASY BLENDING OUR VOICES
WHEN WE'RE OFFERED SO MANY CHOICES!
IF IT'S HARD TO FOLLOW ALONG...

THEO/IRIS/KICKER.
JUST SING

BRETT/JOANNA.
(Echoing)
SING, SING

THEO/IRIS/KICKER.
A SIMPLE

BRETT/JOANNA.
(Echoing)
A SIMPLE

JOANNA.
CHANUKAH

IRIS.
CHRISTMAS

THEO.
KWANZAA

KICKER.
SANTA CLAUS

KICKER/THEO.
HOLIDAY

IRIS/JOANNA.
HOLY DAY

BRETT.
(Exasperated)
PEACE ON EARTH!

ALL.
SONG!!!

(After the "button" of the number, all but JOANNA and IRIS exit.)

(A title appears:)

[Girl Hates Boy - But Not Really]

IRIS. *(Spotting BRETT'S scarf on the stage.)* Look, Brett's scarf!
JOANNA. Let me see!

(She takes it and nuzzles it lovingly.)

IRIS. D'ya think he knows you like him?
JOANNA. I hope not.
IRIS. I'll be happy to tell him.
JOANNA. No.
IRIS. I'll just sorta let it slip out...
JOANNA. Iris! No!!
IRIS. ...real subtle, like, ya know, *(YELLS)* "Brett?! Joanna thinks you're really cute!"
JOANNA. I would DIE!
IRIS. So what're you gonna do? Let somebody else grab him?
JOANNA. I don't know. Maybe he knows already. But if he DOES know, he hasn't given me the slightest hint, which can only mean he absolutely hates my guts.
IRIS. Okay. I'll tell him. *(YELLS)* Brett! *I* think you're cute!
JOANNA. *(Giving IRIS a friendly shove.)* Good-BYE!
IRIS. He knows. *(EXITING)* Trust me. He knows!! *(SHE is gone.)*
JOANNA. Dear God,
Are boys better than girls? I know you are one, but try to be fair.

Song: *"SIX HOURS AS A PRINCESS"*

JOANNA.
CINDERELLA HAD HER GODMOTHER,
BUT I'M LUCKY I HAVE YOU.
SO MAYBE I DON'T NEED A GLASS SHOE
TO MAKE MY WISH COME TRUE...

I WANT SIX HOURS AS A PRINCESS —
I'D TAKE FIVE OR EVEN THREE.

YES, THREE HOURS AS A PRINCESS,
JUST THE TWO OF US — BRETT AND ME.

AND WE'LL TALK ABOUT HOPES AND DREAMS,
NOT SPORTS — IMAGINE THAT!
AND SOON I'LL FIND WHAT'S ON HIS MIND
AND UNDERNEATH THAT HAT.

I WANT ONE HOUR AS A PRINCESS.
DON'T YOU THINK THAT I'M ALLOWED
JUST ONE HOUR AS A PRINCESS?
OKAY, TEN MINUTES - I'M NOT PROUD!

AND THE NIGHT WILL BE FILLED WITH STARS,
AND HE'LL BE HOLDING MY HAND.
AND BRETT WILL SAY HE CARES FOR ME
'CAUSE THAT'S WHAT YOU'LL COMMAND.

THEN FINALLY THE GIRL I HOPE TO BE
WILL MAGICALLY APPEAR.
GOD, YOU CAN MAKE MY DREAM COME TRUE —
(JOANNA sits on a bench).
JUST SEND ME A SIGN
TO LET ME KNOW YOU'RE HERE.

(BRETT enters performing yo-yo feats – or some other trick that displays virtuosity, like juggling sock balls or dribbling a basketball. This is the sign that JOANNA wanted. She looks up to God and mouths "thank you." KICKER sneaks-in and hides behind the bench JOANNA is sitting on.)

BRETT. ...798 ...799...800...801...802...803...804...

(JOANNA reads, pretending to ignore BRETT, who continues counting and performing his trick. JOANNA turns pages extra loud to get his attention and he goofs up.)

BRETT. Um ... do you have to sit there?
JOANNA. It's a free country.

BRETT. Not to sit on a bench and turn pages so loud you make a person who's trying to get into the Guinness Book of World records mess up!

JOANNA. Sorry, but you don't own every bench in the universe.

BRETT. *(Points off in the distance.)* There's a bench over there you can sit on.

JOANNA. I like this bench better. *(Pause)*

BRETT. *(Frustrated, he resumes his trick and begins his count all over.)* 1...2... 3...

JOANNA. Hey, why do you have all these things on your hat?

(She leans close to his hat and peers intently at the buttons.)

BRETT. Forget about it, okay?

JOANNA. What's your problem?

BRETT. I don't have a problem!

JOANNA. Well, you're acting kind of like...weird.

BRETT. Yeah? Well you'd feel weird too, if your father was gonna move to Wyoming which is about eight million miles away!

(BRETT charges off. KICKER sneezes from behind the bench.)

JOANNA. *(Furious)* Kicker Brown!

KICKER. *(With mock innocence.)* Hi, Joanna...

JOANNA. What are you doing here?!! *(KICKER giggles.)* Whatever you saw, you better keep your little mouth shut. Now go home and clean your room!

KICKER. It is clean!

JOANNA. Then clean it again!

KICKER. Dear God...Well, I did what I promised. But you did not send me the pony yet. What about it?

JOANNA. Kicker, vanish!!

KICKER. What's your problem?!

JOANNA. Brett Williams is an idiot! I'll never speak to him again as long as I live!

KICKER. You'll *have* to speak to him *(Sassy, wiggling his butt.)* if you wanna marry him.

JOANNA. *(In a rage)* OHHHHHH! You're really gonna get it when you get home!

(She exits fast.)

Song: *"AN ONLY CHILD"*

KICKER.
Dear God...
IF ONLY YOU COULD MAKE ME AN ONLY CHILD –
I'D GET TO TELL MY SISTER TO GO...
SHE WOULDN'T HOG THE BATHROOM,
I'D HAVE THE BIGGER BEDROOM,
THEN MAYBE I'D HAVE ROOM TO GROW.

AN ONLY CHILD IS NEVER A LONELY CHILD –
NOT WHEN HE'S SURROUNDED BY TOYS
PLUS A PONY AND A PUPPY,
A RABBIT AND A GUPPY...
AS LONG AS ALL MY PETS ARE BOYS!

GOD, I'M SURE YOU HAVE A LOT OF PRAYERS TO GRANT
FROM JERUSALEM TO WASHINGTON TO ROME
'CAUSE ALL THE WORLD IS PRAYING FOR WORLD PEACE...
BUT SHOULDN'T PEACE BEGIN AT HOME?!

LIFE WOULD BE SO COOL AS AN ONLY CHILD,
NO ONE TATTLES WHEN YOU DO WRONG.
SAY GOODBYE TO FIGHTING

JOANNA.
(Entering)
PULLING HAIR AND BITING

KICKER.
HEY, THIS IS S'PPOSED TO BE *MY* SONG!

JOANNA.
FINE.
SO I GUESS I WON'T PLAY YOU MY COOL MUSIC.

KICKER.
AND I GUESS I WON'T SHOW YOU MY COOL ANT FARM.

JOANNA.
AND I WON'T CLIMB A TREE TO FREE YOUR KITE

KICKER.
OR TELL KNOCK-KNOCK JOKES IN THE MIDDLE OF THE NIGHT

JOANNA.
OR TEACH YOU NOT TO WEAR THOSE DORKY CLOTHES

KICKER.
OR HOW TO SPRAY MILK OUT OF YOUR NOSE!

JOANNA.
OR SWEAR

KICKER.
OR BURP

JOANNA.
OR EAT LIKE A HOG

KICKER.
OR MAKE A SMELLY...

JOANNA/KICKER.
PFHEWWWW!!!
(They make a "Fart" noise or "Raspberry")
AND BLAME IT ON THE DOG!!!

(They explode with laughter.)

KICKER.
WELL, I GUESS I REALLY CAN'T BE AN ONLY CHILD...

JOANNA.
I'M HERE, SO IT'S SORT OF TOO LATE.

KICKER.
WELL, IT'S REALLY NOT SO BAD

JOANNA.
IN FACT, I'M KIND OF GLAD

JOANNA/KICKER.
TO HAVE
SOMEONE TO...

HATE!!!!!!

(Transition of lights and music. A title appears:)

[Who's In Charge?]

THEO. *(Enters as a spy and covertly snatches a cookie jar. He opens the jar and inhales deeply.)* Mmm. The heavenly smell of fresh cookies. *(As his mother.)* "No cookie for you, Theo." *(As himself.)* Mom, I have to have a cookie! Right now! Or I'll die! *(As his mother.)* "Not before dinner." *(As himself.)* Why can't we have a chocolate dinner?

(THEO reaches into the cookie jar and pulls out a cookie.)

MOTHER'S VOICE. *(Off stage.)* Theo - drop that cookie!

(He drops it into the jar.)

Song: *"WHEN I AM IN CHARGE"*

THEO.
NOW HOW DID SHE KNOW?
(To God:)
DID SHE HEAR IT FROM YOU?
IT'S NOT FAIR THAT SHE CAN TELL JUST WHAT I'LL DO.
GOD, IF YOU GIVE GROWN-UPS SPECIAL POWERS,
THEN I WISH YOU'D GIVE US KIDS SOME POWER TOO...

KICKER. Dear God, If you made the rule for kids to take out the garbage, please change it.

JOANNA. When I'm a mother and my kids ask me why they can't stay up late, I'll never tell them "because I said so."

(We hear a cacophony of parents' voices.)

PARENT'S VOICES. *(Overlapping:)*
Turn down that so-called music!
There will be no T.V. till you finish your homework...
I want this room picked up! Now!
We will not have that language in this house!
You will not leave the house in that shirt!
Chew with your mouth closed...
What did you just say, young lady?

THEO.
WHEN I AM IN CHARGE
I'LL HAVE IT MY WAY...

IRIS.
MY CHORES WILL BE REPLACED
BY A DAY OF FREE PLAY.

JOANNA.
THE GAME "MOTHER MAY I?"
WILL BE "MOTHER HAS NO SAY"

IRIS/THEO/JOANNA.
WHEN I AM IN CHARGE!

BRETT.
WHEN I AM IN CHARGE
I'LL KNOW HOW IT FEELS...

KICKER.
TO ONLY EAT DESSERTS
IN BETWEEN "HAPPY MEALS."

IRIS.
I'LL RAISE MY ALLOWANCE

KICKER.
AND LOWER STEERING WHEELS

BRETT/IRIS/KICKER.
WHEN I AM IN CHARGE!

ALL.
JUST ONCE I'D LIKE TO DO AS I LIKE
AND WEAR WHATEVER I LIKE TO WEAR
AND EAT WHATEVER I LIKE TO EAT
AND NEVER NEVER NEVER HAVE TO SHARE!

JOANNA.
WHEN I AM IN CHARGE
BRETT WON'T BE A JERK —
HE'LL HOLD MY HAND IN HOMEROOM
AND DO MY HOMEWORK.

THEO.
I'LL LUNCH WITH CAPTAIN CRUNCH

KICKER.
AND FLY WITH CAPTAIN KIRK

ALL.
WHEN I AM IN CHARGE!

IRIS.
WHEN I AM IN CHARGE
I'LL TAKE UP THE DRUMS

KICKER.
I'LL PLAY MY MUSIC LOUD

BRETT.
AND TATTOO BOTH MY THUMBS.

KICKER.
I'LL FORM MY OWN BAND

AND CALL IT "KICKER AND THE BUMS"

ALL.
WHEN I AM IN CHARGE!
OH, WHY SHOULD FREEDOM TAKE FOREVER?
WHY DO WE HAVE TO WAIT TILL WE'RE GROWN?
WHY CAN'T WE PACK OUR THINGS AND MOVE OUT?
HEY, WHY NOT LIVE TOGETHER ON OUR OWN?

BRETT. Just think of it...
NO ONE TO SAY "GO TO BED"

THEO.
"YOU FORGOT TO BRUSH YOUR TEETH"

IRIS.
"THE CAT WASN'T FED"

ALL.
THERE ARE THINGS WE'D RATHER DO INSTEAD...

BRETT.
LIKE POURING PEPSI ON MY WHEATIES

THEO.
HAVIN' PIZZA EVERY NIGHT

KICKER.
TRASH MY ROOM

JOANNA.
AND WHENEVER I LIKE IT –

ALL.
A PILLOW FIGHT!

JOANNA.
I'M LEAVING ON THE TELEVISION

THEO.
HANGIN' OUT

KICKER.
STAYING UP REAL LATE

ALL.
EVERY NIGHT'S A PARTY
WITH A TON OF FRIENDS AND –

JOANNA.
WAIT!
WE'LL NEED TO SHOP FOR FOOD
TO FEED EVERY FRIEND.

KICKER.
BUT HOW DO WE GET THERE?

IRIS.
AND WHAT'LL WE SPEND?

BRETT.
WE'VE NO JOB

IRIS.
NO ALLOWANCE

THEO.
NO WHEELS

KICKER.
'CEPT A BIKE.

JOANNA.
I CAN BARELY BOIL WATER —

BRETT.
STILL, WE'LL DO AS WE LIKE!

IRIS.
BUT WHO WILL DO LAUNDRY

JOANNA.
OR PAY FOR THE PHONE...

ALL.
OR KISS US GOODNIGHT WHEN WE'RE LIVING ALONE?

IRIS.
WHEN I AM IN CHARGE,

JOANNA.
THAT DAY WILL BE GREAT.

KICKER.
FOR NOW I'LL BE A KID —
SO I'LL STAY AT HOME PLATE.

BRETT.
I GUESS I'M A ROOKIE

THEO.
SO THIS COOKIE BETTER WAIT
TILL I AM IN CHARGE...

(THEO returns the cookie to the cookie jar.)

    MOTHER'S VOICE. *(From offstage.)* Thank you, Theo.
    THEO. *(Ostentatiously)* You're welcome, mom.

ALL.
WHEN I AM IN CHARGE!
YEAH!

(End Of Act I)

ACT II

(A title appears:)

[Dreams & Wishes]

(KICKER and IRIS enter carrying books. She's buoyant, has exchanged black turtleneck for bright colors.)

    KICKER. Hey, Iris, how come you're not sad anymore?
    IRIS. Life goes on. I got a pony.
    KICKER. *(Shocked)* You got a pony? A real pony?
    IRIS. Yep.
    KICKER. Wow! You must have a really clean room!

(BRETT and JOANNA enter; her arms are full of books. He has backpack on one shoulder.)

    BRETT. Lotta books there. Lemme carry 'em for you.
    JOANNA. Thanks. I'm fine.
    IRIS. You can carry mine if you want.

(JOANNA gives her a look.)

    THEO. *(Enters, carrying mitt and books and wearing a hat, Brett-style.)* Hey, Brett, will you coach me after school?
    BRETT. Can't. Basketball game.
    IRIS. I hope you guys win.
    JOANNA. Me, too.
    THEO. Me, three.
    BRETT. Man, I sure hope so.

THEO. *(Offers BRETT his hat.)* If you wear my new lucky hat...
BRETT. Thanks, buddy, but...*(Doesn't take it.)*
THEO. ...then you can't lose!
BRETT. Maybe. But, like, ya never know.
IRIS. It's in the stars. You will win.
JOANNA. I'd be there, but unfortunately I have to baby-sit my angelic little brother.
IRIS. *I'll* be there!

(The sound of a school bell indicates the end of recess. The KIDS move to their "classrooms," jabbering happily.)

TEACHER'S VOICE. Silence! This is a classroom not a Zoo. Now, open your books and turn to chapter nine.

Song: *"DAYDREAMS"*

ALL.
DAYDREAMS
LIFT ME UP
WHEN I'M STUCK IN SCHOOL...

JOANNA. Dear God, I wish I was a teacher so I could boss people around — like Ms. Nedermeyer!
THEO. Dear God, Our teacher told us to write to our favorite person so I am writing to you even though you can't write back, and you're not a person.
KICKER. Dear God, Second grade is even harder than first grade. I hope this doesn't keep going on and on...

JOANNA/IRIS.
I WILL NOT DREAM IN CLASS
I WILL NOT DREAM IN CLASS
I WILL NOT DREAM OF BRETT WILLIAMS
WHO SITS SO NEAR WE BREATHE
THE SAME AIR EVERY SINGLE DAY...

JOANNA.
EXCEPT ON WEEKENDS WHEN WE DON'T HAVE SCHOOL

IRIS.
LIKE, WOW, HE'S COOLER THAN COOL!

JOANNA.
SO HOW COME WITH ME HE'S ALWAYS HOT OR COLD?
I'D LIKE TO KNOW BEFORE I'M AN OLD MAID —
ONE WHO NEVER HAS FUN
WHO TEACHES THE SIXTH GRADE
AND WEARS HER HAIR IN A BUN

JOANNA/IRIS.
AND MAKES STUDENTS WRITE ONE
HUNDRED TIMES,
"I WILL NOT DREAM IN CLASS

ADD BRETT/KICKER.
I WILL NOT DREAM IN CLASS

ADD THEO.
I WILL NOT DREAM IN CLASS..."

ALL.
DAYDREAMS
DREAMS YOU DREAM
WHEN YOUR EYES DON'T CLOSE —

KICKER.
FAST CARS

THEO.
EXPLORING MARS

IRIS.
GETTING A NEW NOSE.

JOANNA.
BOYS WITH LOVELY MANNERS

BRETT.
GIRLS IN SKIMPY CLOTHES

ALL.
ARE PART OF
DAYDREAMS
PLAY DREAMS
THAT NO ONE ELSE KNOWS...

THEO.
I WILL NOT DREAM IN CLASS
I WILL NOT DREAM IN CLASS...

Dear God...
ARE YOU HAPPY WITH ME?
DID I TURN OUT LIKE YOU HOPED I WOULD?
AM I DOING GOOD?
(Corrects himself.)
AM I DOING *WELL?*
CONFESS.
(He waits for an answer.)
I THINK I'LL TAKE YOUR SILENCE FOR A YES!

IRIS.
WHAT DO YOU HAVE PLANNED FOR ME
WHEN I'M ALL GROWN?

THEO.
AN ATHLETE

IRIS.
DOCTOR

KICKER.
ASTRONAUT

THEO/IRIS/KICKER.
WITH CHILDREN OF MY OWN?

ALL.
WHAT IF ALL THE DREAMS INSIDE DO NOT COME
TRUE?
WILL I DISAPPOINT —

BRETT.
MY PARENTS

JOANNA.
TEACHERS

IRIS.
ME

KICKER.
YOU?

ALL.
I WILL NOT DREAM IN CLASS
I WILL NOT DREAM IN CLASS...

BRETT.
WHY WYOMING?!
WHY DID HE MOVE TO WYOMING?
AND NOW MY DAD'LL
BE SURROUNDED BY CATTLE
A MILLION LIGHT YEARS AWAY.
FOR HE BOUGHT A HOME
WHERE THE BUFFALO ROAM
AND MY SKIES ARE NOW CLOUDY ALL DAY ...

("DAY" is sung simultaneously with "DAY" of DAYDREAMS.)

ALL. *(Except BRETT.)*
DAYDREAMS

ALL.
DREAMS YOU DREAM
WHEN YOU'RE HALF AWAKE:

KICKER.
STEEL GUITARS

IRIS.
MOVIE STARS

THEO.
DRINKING A MILKSHAKE.

JOANNA.
HAVING CURVES LIKE BARBIE

BRETT.
BARBIE FIVE-FOOT-THREE!

ALL.
ARE PART OF DAYDREAMS
PLAYDREAMS
ALL A PART OF ME...
ALL A PART OF ME...
ALL A PART OF —

(Dramatic transition of lighting. Baseball music sounds.)

ALL. *(But THEO.)*
Play ball!

(We hear the crack of a bat.)

THEO. *(Rushing to catch the ball with his mitt.)* I got it! I got it!...

(The kids form a group chanting THEO'S name.)

ALL. *(But THEO.)*
THEO! THEO! THEEE —

(THEO backs up to catch the ball and misses.)

ALL. *(But THEO.)*
(Disappointed)
OHHHHH!

(They exit.)

Song: *"KICKER BROWN"*

THEO.
EVERY DAY DURING RECESS
WE COMPETE IN SOME GRIM SPORTS.
IN BASEBALL OR SOCCER
OR GYMNASTICS,
I AM VOTED KING OF SPASTICS!
WHAT'S MORE I LOOK SILLY IN GYM SHORTS.

AND MY PARENTS INSIST I'M A CLOSET JOCK —
WELL, ONLY IN THEIR DREAMS!
I ALWAYS WANNA QUIT
EACH TIME WE SPLIT INTO TEAMS.

AFTER THE CAPTAINS HAVE MADE THEIR PICKS
IT ALWAYS COMES DOWN TO JUST TWO:
A MUNCHKIN NAMED KICKER BROWN
AND WELL, GUESS WHO?

    BRETT'S VOICE. *(Begrudgingly)* Hmmm. Theo...Kicker...Theo...Kicker...Theo...Kicker...? *(Sighs)* Theo.

THEO.
THANK YOU, GOD, FOR KICKER BROWN —
I'M SO PLEASED I COULD BURST.
OH, THANK YOU, GOD:
WITH YOUR HELP
I'M ONLY SECOND WORST!
YES, THANK YOU, GOD,
FOR MAKING KICKER BROWN.

BUT ONE DAY
IN A YEAR OR SO
KICKER'S GONNA GROW,
KICKER'S GONNA GROW!

BEANSTALKS SPROUT
FROM AN EMBRYO.
KICKER'S GONNA GROW,

KICKER'S GONNA GROW!

HE'LL BE AS TALL AS A CHERRY PICKER,
HIS ARMS WILL EXPAND CATCHING FLYBALLS QUICKER.
THOSE KIDS WON'T LOOK AT HIM AND SNICKER...
THEY'LL BE LAUGHING AT ME —
THAT'S THE KICKER!

(KICKER enters as a ten-foot monster – hoisted on BRETT's shoulders – but we don't see BRETT underneath because KICKER wears an oversized raincoat which covers BRETT. KICKER calls down to tiny THEO:)

KICKER. Hi small fry!

(Laughs uncontrollably, and exits.)

THEO.
(Frightened)
DON'T MAKE ME COME IN LAST.
GOD, I'LL LEAVE IT UP TO YOU
TO THINK OF SOMETHING FAST!

(SFX: A bat hitting a ball.)

IRIS. *(Onstage, hoping to make the catch.)* I got it, I got it! *(Drops the ball.)* Shoot!!

THEO.
OH, THANK YOU, GOD —
YES, THANK YOU, GOD
FOR MAKING
IRIS BURNS!!!!!!!!!!!!!!!!!!!!!!

(A title appears:)

[Boy Likes Girl – Sort Of]

(Lights and music change to BRETT and JOANNA outdoors.)

BRETT. *(Performs a yo-yo trick or spins a basketball on his finger or other show-offy trick.)* Want me to teach you how to do this?

JOANNA. Not really.

BRETT. It's a great thing to know.

JOANNA. I seriously doubt it.

BRETT. That's because you're not a guy.

JOANNA. Thanks for noticing.

BRETT. Guys just naturally know how to do cool stuff like this.

JOANNA. But...does anyone truly care?

BRETT. My dad taught it to me before he...moved away.

(BRETT turns away.)

JOANNA. I guess that must be kind of tough, huh? *(Pause)*

BRETT. What're you looking at?

JOANNA. Um...your hat.

BRETT. What about it?

JOANNA. All those pins! They're great. *(Moving in.)* "Sea World," "Grand Canyon," "Aspen!" Hey, cool!

(Tries to touch it.)

BRETT. *(Furious)* Never touch my hat!

JOANNA. Well pardon me for being interested in your beloved wonderful untouchable...very weird hat!

BRETT. Sorry I yelled at you. It's just...that's all I'm gonna say.

(Starts to exit.)

JOANNA. Fine!

(Sits dejected.)

Song: *"SILLY OLD HAT"*

BRETT.
IT'S JUST A SILLY OLD HAT
THAT I WEAR ON MY HEAD.
IT'S NOT LIKE I CARE ENOUGH

TO WEAR IT TO BED —
'CAUSE I DON'T!

IT'S JUST A SILLY OLD HAT
WITH SOME BUTTONS ATTACHED.
IT'S NOT LIKE I'LL FALL APART
IF IT SHOULD GET SNATCHED,
'CAUSE I WON'T.

IT'S JUST A SILLY OLD HAT
MY FATHER BOUGHT AT A GAME.
THE YANKEES WERE TAKING A WHIPPING
AND DAD SAID HE AND MOM WERE SLIPPING, TOO.

"KID, SOMETIMES MARRIAGES FAIL...
IT'S KIND OF LIKE SCHOOL — YOU GET GRADED.
AND JUST LIKE A SHORTSTOP THAT'S GETTING STALE,
FATHERS ALSO GET TRADED."

IT'S JUST A SILLY OLD HAT
THAT I WEAR WITH MY DAD.
IT'S NOT LIKE I SEE HIM MUCH
BUT DON'T GET ALL SAD —
'CAUSE I'M NOT.

BUT STILL WE TRAVEL A LOT,
THERE'S A PIN FOR EACH TRIP –
TO MAINE OR TO DISNEYLAND,
SOME COOL BATTLESHIP.
SEE THIS SPOT?

SO BIG DEAL
HE'S NOT THERE
WHEN I WAKE UP MOST DAYS
OR COME HOME AFTER SCHOOL
OR HAVE PROBLEMS WITH MATH
OR GET READY FOR BED...

I'VE GOT THIS SILLY OLD HAT
THAT I WEAR ON MY HEAD.

(JOANNA takes BRETT'S hand. Transition of lights and music. A title appears:)

[Help Wanted]

THEO. *(With a large photo of himself, a 5x7 envelope, a mitt, and a baseball.)* Dear God, I don't think you were listening when I asked you to make me a better player. I'm sending my picture so you'll know who I am. Theo! *(THEO places the picture in the envelope and seals it. Seeing BRETT enter hurriedly, THEO puts on his mitt.)* Hey, Brett, will you coach me now?

BRETT. Well, actually, Theo, I got a lotta stuff to do.

THEO. What about my "Birthday Bonus"? Remember? You said?

BRETT. *(Beat)* Oh. Right. *(Holds hand out)* Toss it to me. Keep your eye on the ball. *(BRETT tosses the ball to THEO. He misses it.)* It's okay. It's okay. *(THEO clumsily tosses the ball back to BRETT.)* Try it again, but this time try catching it *in* the mitt.

(BRETT tosses the ball to THEO and he catches it!)

THEO. *(In awe.)* OOOOOooohhh!

(He tosses the ball back.)

BRETT. See! Okay, try it again.

(BRETT tosses the ball and THEO catches it.)

THEO. *(Still in awe.)* Awesome! And after we're done, can I help you with your...stuff?

BRETT. Thanks, but nobody can help.

THEO. Why not?

BRETT. Because...I'm moving away.

THEO. *(Shocked, stops throwing.)* You're...moving? Where to?
BRETT. Wyoming. But you can't tell anybody yet.
KICKER. *(Entering with IRIS.)* Where's Wyoming?
BRETT. Way out west. I'm gonna be livin' with my dad.
IRIS. Oh, oh! Joanna will fall apart.
KICKER. *(Excited)* Really?
BRETT. Trust me, Joanna's not gonna fall apart.
JOANNA. *(Entering)* Hi. *(They stare at her silently.)* Why're you guys looking so creepy?
KICKER. Brett's moving to Wyoming.
JOANNA. *(To BRETT, shocked.)* WHAT? Is that true?
BRETT. Yeah.
IRIS. C'mon, let's leave them alone.
KICKER. No, I wanna see her fall apart!
THEO. *(Grabs KICKER.)* C'mon Kicker.
KICKER. *(As he exits.)* I wanna see her fall apart.
JOANNA. How come you didn't tell me?
BRETT. I just found out two hours ago.
JOANNA. I mean, why? What happened?
BRETT. Nothin'. Just, my dad said, do I want to come to Wyoming and live with him. So, y'know, I'm gonna.
JOANNA. Are you mad at your mom or something?
BRETT. No. It's just, I haven't been seein' my dad that much lately, so, like...*(JOANNA covers her eyes to hide her tears.)* Aw, come on, Joanna, I'll be back to see my mom...a lot...because, you know, I'm gonna miss her — and you guys — like crazy. You okay?
JOANNA. *(Unconvincingly)* Yeah. Why wouldn't I be?

(He places his hat on her head. She touches it.)

BRETT. I gotta go pack.

(He exits.)

Song: *"SIX HOURS AS A PRINCESS (REPRISE)"*

JOANNA.
AND THE NIGHT WILL BE FILLED WITH STARS,
AND HE'LL BE HOLDING MY HAND.

AND BRETT WILL SAY HE CARES FOR ME
'CAUSE THAT'S WHAT YOU'LL COMMAND.

    JOANNA. *(Spoken)* Dear God, You better make all the bad things go away or you won't get elected next time!

(Pin-spots pick out IRIS and KICKER.)

    KICKER. Dear God, How come — if you are really God and you know everything bad before it happens — why do you let it happen?
    IRIS. Dear God, What kind of a world is it where so many terrible things happen? Maybe you better start it all over again.

(As the music for "How Come?" begins we see BRETT packing his things.)

Song: *"HOW COME?!"*

THEO.
HOW COME MY FRIEND IS MOVING AWAY?

KICKER.
HOW COME MY SISTER'S BOSSY ALL DAY?

JOANNA.
HOW COME SOMETIMES I JUST WANNA CRY?

BRETT.
HOW COME IT'S ROTTEN SAYING GOODBYE?

ALL.
WHAT'S TO GAIN
IN FEELING PAIN
WHEN FEELING GOOD IS GREAT?
HOW COME...

KICKER.
I'LL SOON HAVE TO DATE?

JOANNA.
HOW COME YOU BLESS US AFTER EACH SNEEZE
BUT YOU DON'T PUT AN END TO DISEASE?

KICKER.
HOW COME I'VE TROUBLE TYING MY SHOES?

BRETT.
HOW COME IT'S NEVER EASY TO CHOOSE?

JOANNA.
BOMBS EXPLODE

THEO.
AND ROCKY ROAD I'M NOT SUPPOSED TO EAT.

ALL.
HOW COME...

IRIS.
I'VE GOT SMELLY FEET?

THEO.
HOW COME EVERY CAT HAS NINE LIVES BUT MINE?

BRETT.
HOW COME YOU INVENTED DIVORCE?

JOANNA.
BRETT'S NEVER SENT ME A VALENTINE?

KICKER.
AND I STILL DO NOT OWN A HORSE?!!

IRIS.
HOW COME IN SCHOOL I GOTTA LEARN FRENCH?

THEO.
HOW COME IN SPORTS I JUST WARM THE BENCH?

JOANNA.
HOW COME SOME COUNTRIES SUFFER FROM DROUGHT?

KICKER.
HOW COME MY TONSILS HAVE TO COME OUT?

BRETT.
PEOPLE SWEAR

JOANNA.
AND WHERE'S CLEAN AIR?

KICKER.
AND THERE'S NO DINOSAURS.

ALL.
HOW COME THERE'LL ALWAYS BE WARS?

IRIS.
HOW COME ALL MY TEETH ARE LOADED WITH PLAQUE?

THEO.
HOW COME I DON'T HAVE PERFECT SIGHT?

JOANNA/KICKER/IRIS.
HOW COME YOU MADE COLORS IN EVERY SHADE...

ALL.
BUT SOME ONLY SEE BLACK AND WHITE?!

IRIS/BRETT/THEO.
HOW COME SOME NEVER LEARN RIGHT FROM WRONG?

KICKER/JOANNA.
HOW COME SOME COUNTRIES CAN'T GET ALONG?

IRIS/BRETT/THEO.
HOW COME SOME PEOPLE GET REALLY SICK?

ALL.
WE NEED SOME ANSWERS DOUBLE QUICK!
DO YOU CARE
THAT LIFE'S UNFAIR?
IT MEANS A LOT TO SOME.
WE NEED TO KNOW RIGHT NOW
WHY ALL THIS YOU ALLOW!

BRETT.
HOW

IRIS.
HOW

THEO.
HOW

KICKER.
HOW

JOANNA.
HOW

(BRETT exits with his duffle bag.)

ALL. *(Except BRETT)*
HOW COME!!!!!!!!!!!!!!!!!!!

(A title appears:)

[Approvals and Thanks]

(Transition to night. JOANNA, IRIS and THEO carry lit flashlights. KICKER follows them.)

JOANNA. I just can't believe Brett Williams will be gone tomorrow. Forever!
IRIS. It is very strange.
KICKER. It's dopey!
THEO. My best baseball buddy.

JOANNA. It's not fair!
IRIS. Don'tcha think he'll also miss us?
JOANNA. I sure hope so.
THEO. Me, too.
KICKER. He's the only really big guy that knows my name.
JOANNA. I feel like crying.
THEO. Me, too, kinda.
IRIS. Yeah, but see, for Brett...it's okay...because he's happy he's going to live with his father again.
KICKER. So when we see him, do we hafta act all fakey and pretend we're happy?
IRIS. Yes.
THEO. Okay.
JOANNA. *(Looking at her watch.)* Oh. OH! Move guys! We were supposed to meet him about 3 seconds ago!
KICKER. Owww! Dumb stupid rock!
JOANNA. What's your problem, Kicker?
KICKER. OUCH! I can't see anything! Dear God, You should leave the sun out at night when we need it the most.
JOANNA. Turn on your flashlight, Munchkin!
KICKER. Oh yeah.
JOANNA. And hurry! We're late!

(Stars gradually begin to appear as they arrive at the prescribed meeting place.)

THEO. He isn't here.
JOANNA. Brett?
IRIS. I don't see him anywhere.
KICKER. Maybe he drank some stuff that made him invisible!
IRIS. What if he forgot and doesn't show up?
JOANNA. Well, then I guess I'll have to kill him.
KICKER. Really?
JOANNA. He'll be here. I just know it.

(Pause)

BRETT. *(Enters with a flashlight.)* Yo! Sorry I'm late...I got held up.

JOANNA. Thank you, God.

BRETT. Y'know, tearful mom and all.

KICKER. Joanna said she was gonna kill you if you didn't show up!

BRETT. I know. That's why I came.

IRIS. It is really beautiful out tonight. Isn't it Brett?

BRETT. Yeah, great...except I'm not gonna be together with you guys for a long time.

IRIS. *(To distract the group from their sadness.)* Look, everybody, there's the Big Dipper! Isn't it awesome?

THEO. Yeah, awesome!

(Music in.)

JOANNA. I love the Big Dipper — because when you look at the stars in it, they seem like they must be...friends.

BRETT. I was just thinking that.

JOANNA. ...and if they could talk...I bet they'd say how great it is to...to always be together, forever, to be part of the same famous shape that people have been looking at since the beginning of time...but, actually, each one of those stars is millions and skadillions of light years apart, so they don't even know they form a pattern, they don't even know they're, like, like...

BRETT. ...like us?

JOANNA. Yeah...like us!...Brett?

BRETT. Yeah?

JOANNA. ...see that star?

BRETT. *(Looks up.)* Which one?

JOANNA. *(Points to it.)* Right above the water tank on top of that building?

BRETT. Where? Oh yeah, now I see it.

JOANNA. I wished on it.

BRETT. What'd you wish?

JOANNA. Something...

BRETT. What...?

JOANNA. It's a secret.

BRETT. Come on. You can tell me!

JOANNA. NO! You can't tell anybody, or else it won't come true.

KICKER. She wants you to get her a baby!

JOANNA. *(Mortified, JOANNA stares at her brother.)* Brett...? The first night...when you're in Wyoming?

BRETT. Wyoming! That sounds so strange.

JOANNA. Go outside and look up in the sky for the Big Dipper. Like, at 8 o'clock sharp, okay?

BRETT. What will that prove?

IRIS. Well, back here, it will be...ten o'clock, because of the time difference —

JOANNA. *(JOANNA shoots her a look.)* Anyway, we'll all come out, and we'll be looking at the Big Dipper right when you are, see...

IRIS. That will be so cool!

THEO. So then you and us, we'll be looking at the same stars at the same time...

JOANNA. ...then we'll be, like, connected. So you'll know we're thinking of you.

BRETT. Yeah. Right. I bet!
IRIS. Really! It'll work.
THEO. Do it, Brett! *(Simultaneously)*
JOANNA. You have to!
KICKER. It'll be awesome!

BRETT. Wait, will you guys really do it?

IRIS. Yeah!

JOANNA. We promise.

(Musical chord.)

IRIS. Dear God, I saw a falling star. *(Beat)* You should be more careful.

JOANNA. Dear God, I wished on a star twice, but nothing happened. Now what?

THEO. Dear God, It's great how you get all the stars in the right places.

BRETT. Dear God, If you do all the things everybody says you do, you must be pretty busy. So here's my question: When is the best time I can talk to you? They say you are always listening, but when will you be listening over Jackson Hole, Wyoming?

Song: *"I KNOW"*

BRETT.
I'VE HEARD PEOPLE SAY

THE WORLD CAN BE EXPLAINED
BY ATOMS COLLIDING.

    JOANNA.
AND THEN SOME INSIST
IF GOD REALLY DOES EXIST,
WELL, HE MUST BE HIDING.

    THEO.
I SAY LET THE DOUBTERS DOUBT

    ALL.
'CAUSE, GOD, I FOUND YOU OUT...

    KICKER.
EVERY TIME I COUNT THE STARS IN THE SKY,
I KNOW.

    IRIS.
OR WATCH A SINGLE CLOUD SAIL LAZILY BY,
I KNOW.

    THEO.
WHO ELSE COULD MAKE THE GRAND CANYON
OH, SO GRAND

    BRETT.
OR FILL A SEASHORE UP WITH TINY GRAINS OF
SAND

(BRETT takes JOANNA'S hand.)

    JOANNA.
OR MAKE THE FEELING THAT I GET FROM HOLDING
YOUR HAND?

    ALL.
I KNOW, I KNOW

THEO.
I'VE HEARD PEOPLE SNEER
IF GOD IS REALLY HERE,
HE'S AN UNDERACHIEVER.

IRIS.
WELL, THIS IS WHAT I'VE FOUND
IF THEY TAKE A LOOK AROUND...

KICKER.
...THEY'LL BE A BELIEVER.

JOANNA.
FOR YOU ARE HERE IN EVERYTHING,

ALL.
EVEN IN THIS SONG WE SING.

THEO/BRETT.
EVERY TIME I CATCH THE SUNRISE AT DAWN,
I KNOW

(They execute a perfect "High-Five")

THEO/KICKER.
OR SEE AN UGLY DUCKLING CHANGE TO A SWAN,
I KNOW.

BRETT/IRIS.
WHO ELSE COULD HELP THE BALD EAGLE FLY
SO HIGH

KICKER/JOANNA.
OR LET MY SPIRITS SOAR WHEN EATING APPLE PIE

ALL.
OR MAKE A BETTER WORLD WITH JUST
A BUTTERFLY?
I KNOW, I KNOW.

EVERY TIME I SEE A TREE STANDING TALL, I KNOW,
OR WHEN MAPLE LEAVES CHANGE COLOR IN FALL, I KNOW.
I HAVE SO MANY QUESTIONS TO ASK OF YOU,
YOU ANSWER EVERY ONE IN EVERYTHING YOU DO...

IRIS
IN THE SKY

Add KICKER.
IN THE SEA

Add JOANNA.
IN THE RAIN

Add THEO.
IN THE SNOW

Add BRETT.
IN THE LIGHT
YES, I KNOW...
IN THE STARS,
NOW I KNOW.

ALL.
IN THE SKY
IN THE SEA
IN THE RAIN
IN THE SNOW
IN THE LIGHT
YES, I KNOW...

IN MY HEART,
NOW I KNOW.

(End Of Play)

(At the end of the bows, the cast reprises "I KNOW" and encourages the audience to clap to the song in rhythm...)

Song: *"I KNOW" (reprise)*

ALL.
EVERY TIME I SEE A TREE STANDING TALL, I KNOW,
OR WHEN MAPLE LEAVES CHANGE COLOR IN FALL, I KNOW.
I HAVE SO MANY QUESTIONS TO ASK OF YOU,
YOU ANSWER EVERY ONE IN EVERYTHING YOU DO...

IN THE SKY
IN THE SEA
IN THE RAIN
IN THE SNOW
IN THE LIGHT
YES, I KNOW...

IN MY HEART,
NOW I KNOW!

PROP LIST

Kicker's Room
Items listed below are for Kicker's drawer:
1 book
4 pieces of clothing
1 pair of binoculars

"Thirteen"
1 Gift bag with baseball glove inside (Brett's gift to Theo)

Theo's Birthday Party
1 small gift-wrapped box (Joanna's gift to Theo)
1 birthday cake with candles on top (Theo's 12th Birthday)
2 gift-wrapped boxes, stacked (gifts for Theo)
1 turtle, pocket sized (Iris' pet turtle Arnold)
1 turtle cage, easy to carry around (Iris)
1 paper/cardboard birthday invitation, pocket sized (Iris' invitation from Theo)

"Questions for the Rain"
1 backpack for Theo (with mini umbrella inside)
1 backpack for Joanna (with mini umbrella inside)
1 backpack for Kicker (with mini umbrella inside)
1 backpack for Brett (with mini umbrella inside)
1 small mesh net for Iris (for catching bugs in water)
1 small plastic container w/1 bug for Joanna (for catching bugs)
1 small plastic container w/3 bugs for Theo (for catching bugs)
several plastic bugs (in water)

"Ants"
1 kickball (for Joanna and Brett)

Post "Ants"
1 black turtleneck for Iris - wardrobe
1 baseball glove for Brett

"Holiday Song"
1 scarf for Iris - wardrobe

CHILDREN'S LETTERS TO GOD

1 scarf for Theo - wardrobe
1 scarf for Kicker - wardrobe
1 scarf for Joanna - wardrobe
1 scarf for Brett - wardrobe
1 African drum (Theo)

Post "Princess"
1 composition notebook with pencil attached (Joanna)
1 yoyo (Brett)

"When I am in Charge"
1 cookie jar with chocolate chip cookies (Theo)

"Daydreams"
1 backpack (Theo)
1 backpack (Joanna)
1 backpack (Kicker)
1 backpack (Brett)
1 backpack (Iris)
1 composition notebook with pencil attached (Theo)
1 composition notebook with pencil attached (Joanna)
1 composition notebook with pencil attached (Kicker)
1 composition notebook with pencil attached (Brett)
1 composition notebook with pencil attached (Iris)
3 hardback subject books (Joanna)
1 baseball glove for Theo (his birthday gift – from earlier scene)
1 baseball hat (similar to Brett's) for Theo

"Kicker Brown"
2 trench coats - 1 each for Brett and Kicker (to cover them up as Kicker is on Brett's shoulders)
1 baseball glove for Iris

Catch Scene
1 picture (with envelope) of Theo
1 baseball
1 baseball glove (from earlier scenes)

"How Come"
1 large duffle bag for Brett - wardrobe
several knick knacks (silly putty, camera, etc) for Brett to pack
5 folded items of clothing for Brett to pack - wardrobe
2 books for Brett to pack
1 light weight jacket for Brett - wardrobe

"I Know"
5 pocket size flashlights, one for each actor (must fit in pockets)